Baritone/Bass

Young Ladies, Shipmates & Journeys

21 Classical Songs for Young Men
Ages Mid-Teens and Up

Compiled by Joan Frey Boytim

ISBN 978-1-4234-3955-4

HAL•LEONARD®
CORPORATION

7777 W. BLUEMOUND RD. P.O. BOX 13819 MILWAUKEE, WI 53213

In Australia Contact:
Hal Leonard Australia Pty. Ltd.
4 Lentara Court
Cheltenham, Victoria, 3192 Australia
Email: ausadmin@halleonard.com.au

Visit Hal Leonard Online at
www.halleonard.com

PREFACE

Young Ladies, Shipmates & Journeys is a classical solo book compiled for male voice students whose changed voices have settled into the tenor and baritone/bass ranges. Accompaniments were recorded by Laura Ward for practice for those who use these learning aids.

This volume, containing 21 songs, complements *The First Book of Tenor and Baritone/Bass Solos, Parts I, II,* and *III.* Even without the words, the listener can definitely tell that the songs are masculine in nature.

Included are some easy English folksongs; however, most of the pieces are robust and rhythmical settings of male texts such as "I Am a Pirate King," "Shipmates o' Mine," "The Song of Brother Hilario," "Nothing But a Plain Old Soldier," and "While the Foaming Billows Roll."

The level of difficulty is easy to medium. Most of the tempos are moderately fast. The ranges are very accessible with a top F for the tenors and only a few high E-flats for the baritones/basses.

Many of the song texts use sailor and sea themes in various forms. The texts regarding young ladies are more in the folksong and classical style rather than sentimental love songs, and are easily presented by younger male singers. One is taken on journeys to various ports of call as well as the old road to home. Adult males as well as teenagers will find many of these pieces pure fun to sing, and a chance to express masculinity in song.

Joan Frey Boytim
May, 2008

CONTENTS

ABOUT THE ENHANCED CD

In addition to piano accompaniments playable on both your CD player and computer, this enhanced CD also includes tempo adjustment and transposition software for computer use only. This software, known as Amazing Slow Downer, was originally created for use in pop music to allow singers and players the freedom to independently adjust both tempo and pitch elements. Because we believe there may be valuable uses for these features in other musical genres, we have included this software as a tool for both the teacher and student. For quick and easy installation instructions of this software, please see below.

In recording a piano accompaniment we necessarily must choose one tempo. Our choice of tempo, phrasing and dynamics is carefully considered. But by the nature of recording, it is only one option. Similar to our choice of tempo, much thought has gone into our choice of key for each song.

However, we encourage you to explore your own interpretive ideas, which may differ from our recordings. This new software feature allows you to adjust the tempo up and down without affecting the pitch. Likewise, Amazing Slow Downer allows you to shift pitch up and down without affecting the tempo. We recommend that these new tempo and pitch adjustment features be used with care and insight.

The audio quality may be somewhat compromised when played through the Amazing Slow Downer. This compromise in quality will not be a factor in playing the CD audio track on a normal CD player or through another audio computer program.

INSTALLATION INSTRUCTIONS:

For Macintosh OS 8, 9 and X:
- Load the CD-ROM into your CD-ROM Drive on your computer.
- Each computer is set up a little differently. Your computer may automatically open the audio CD portion of this enhanced CD and begin to play it.
- To access the CD-ROM features, double-click on the data portion of the CD-ROM (which will have the Hal Leonard icon in red and be named as the book).
- Double-click on the "Amazing OS 8 (9 or X)" folder.
- Double-click "Amazing Slow Downer"/"Amazing X PA" to run the software from the CD-ROM, or copy this file to your hard disk and run it from there.
- Follow the instructions on-screen to get started. The Amazing Slow Downer should display tempo, pitch and mix bars. Click to select your track and adjust pitch or tempo by sliding the appropriate bar to the left or to the right.

For Windows:
- Load the CD-ROM into your CD-ROM Drive on your computer.
- Each computer is set up a little differently. Your computer may automatically open the audio CD portion of this enhanced CD and begin to play it.
- To access the CD-ROM features, click on My Computer then right click on the Drive that you placed the CD in. Click Open. You should then see a folder named "Amazing Slow Downer". Click to open the "Amazing Slow Downer" folder.
- Double-click "setup.exe" to install the software from the CD-ROM to your hard disk. Follow the on-screen instructions to complete installation.
- Go to "Start," "Programs" and find the "Amazing Slow Downer" folder. Go to that folder and select the "Amazing Slow Downer" software.
- Follow the instructions on-screen to get started. The Amazing Slow Downer should display tempo, pitch and mix bars. Click to select your track and adjust pitch or tempo by sliding the appropriate bar to the left or to the right.
- Note: On Windows NT, 2000, XP and Vista, the user should be logged in as the "Administrator" to guarantee access to the CD-ROM drive. Please see the help file for further information.

MINIMUM SYSTEM REQUIREMENTS:

For Macintosh:
Power Macintosh; Mac OS 8.5 or higher; 4 MB Application RAM; 8x Multi-Session CD-ROM drive

For Windows:
Pentium, Celeron or equivalent processor; Windows 95, 98, ME, NT, 2000, XP, Vista; 4 MB Application RAM; 8x Multi-Session CD-ROM drive

BARBARA ALLEN

Words traditional

Old English Melody
arranged by
Roger Quilter

Moderato, poco con moto (♩ = 72)

Lyrics: In Scar - let Town, where I was born, There was a fair maid dwell- in', Made ev - 'ry youth cry "Well - a - day!" Her name was Bar - b'ra Al - len. All in the mer - ry

month of May When green buds they were swel - lin', Young

con tristezza

Jem - my Grove on his death - bed lay For love of Bar - b'ra

Al - len.

Then slow - ly, slow - ly she came up, And

slow - ly she came nigh him, And all she said when __

poco accel.

There she came "Young man, I think you're dy - ing."

poco accel.

mf *con moto*

mp *sonoro*

As

poco dim.

pochiss. rit.

she was walk - ing o'er the fields She heard the dead - bell

sonoro
mp

p

sf

con Ped.

THE BAY OF BISCAY

Andrew Cherry

John Davy

night was drear and dark, Our poor de-vot-ed bark, Till next
cling to slip-p'ry shrouds, Each breath-less sea-man crowds, As she

day there she lay In the Bay of Bis-cay, O!
lay till next day In the Bay of Bis-cay, O!

3. At length the wished for mor-row Broke through the ha-zy sky, Ab -
4. Her yield-ing tim-bers sev-er, Her pitch-y seams are rent, When

BLACKBIRDS AND THRUSHES

Collected and arranged by
Cecil J. Sharp

THE COASTS OF HIGH BARBARY

Collected and arranged by
Cecil J. Sharp

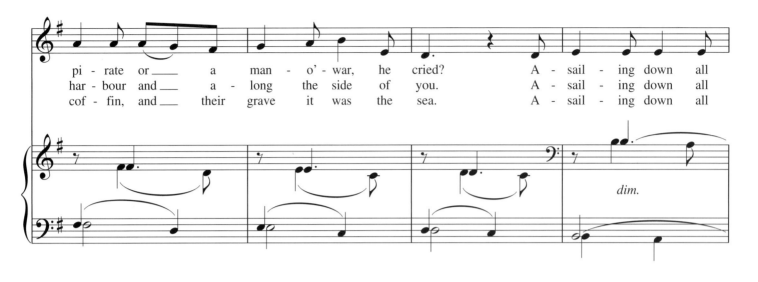

pi - rate or ____ a man - o' - war, he cried? A - sail - ing down all
har - bour and ____ a - long the side of you. A - sail - ing down all
cof - fin, and ____ their grave it was the sea. A - sail - ing down all

on the coasts of High Bar - ba - ry. 3. O are you a
on the coasts of High Bar - ba - ry. 6. For broad - side for
on the coasts of High Bar - ba - ry. 9. But O it was a

pi - rate or man - o' - war, cried we? Blow high! ____ Blow
broad - side, they fought all on the main; Blow high! ____ Blow
cru - el sight and griev - ed us full sore, Blow high! ____ Blow

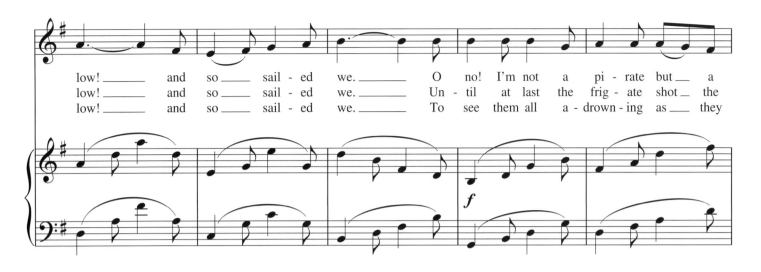

low! ____ and so ____ sail - ed we. ____ O no! I'm not a pi - rate but __ a
low! ____ and so ____ sail - ed we. ____ Un - til at last the frig - ate shot __ the
low! ____ and so ____ sail - ed we. ____ To see them all a - drown - ing as ___ they

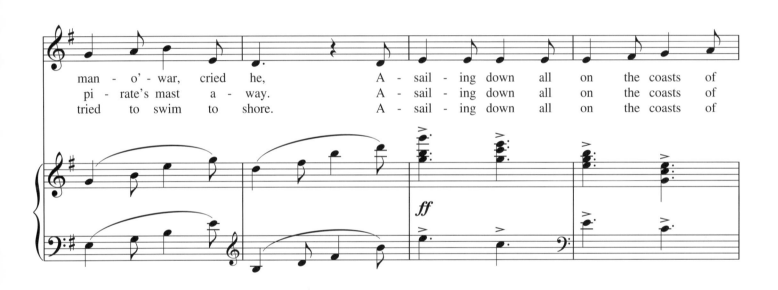

man - o' - war, cried he, A - sail - ing down all on the coasts of
pi - rate's mast a - way. A - sail - ing down all on the coasts of
tried to swim to shore. A - sail - ing down all on the coasts of

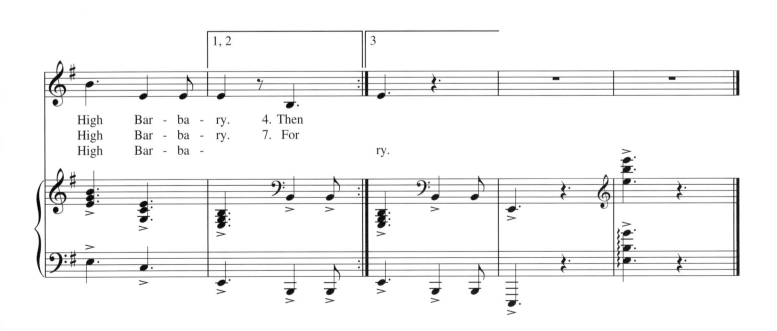

High Bar - ba - ry. 4. Then
High Bar - ba - ry. 7. For
High Bar - ba - ry.

COME LET'S BE MERRY

H. Lane Wilson

'Tis a fol-ly to be sad. For, since the world's gone mad, mad, mad, Why a-lone should we __ be wise, And like dull fools, _____ and like dull fools, _____ like dull fools,_ gaze on oth-er men's joys?

stream _ of life flows on; But when the cheer - ful

day is gone, Still en - deav - our that _ the

next Shall be as gay, _ Shall be as gay, _

be as gay _ and as lit - tle per - plexed.

If you have lei - sure, fol - low pleas - ure, Let not an hour __ of joy pass by;

If you have lei - sure, fol - low pleas - ure, Let not an

THE DUKE OF BEDFORD

Collected and arranged by
Cecil J. Sharp

place he was known _____ And straight a - way to
hunt - men's bare word, _____ Un - til a grand ___
cof - fin of stone, _____ Of the no - ble Duke of

Lon - don To the place _ he was born. 3. They o - pened his
la - dy Cried: _ 'Tis __ my dear lord. 6. She kneeled down be -
Bed - ford In his cof - fin of stone. 9. With - in Wo - burn

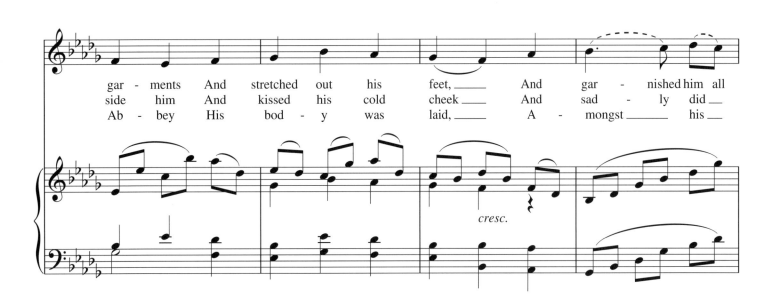

gar - ments And stretched out his feet, _____ And gar - nished him all
side him And kissed his cold cheek _____ And sad - ly did __
Ab - bey His bod - y was laid, _____ A - mongst _____ his

o - ver With _ lil - ies so sweet. 4. 'Twas the 10. And a
mur - mur: My _ poor _ heart will break. 7. For
an - ces - tors, Whose _ deeds are not dead.

weird rush of wa - ters Is heard to this day, _ When a

no - ble Duke of Bed - ford Is _ pass - ing a - way.

FAREWELL, NANCY

Collected and arranged by
Cecil J. Sharp

GENTLE ANNIE

Stephen C. Foster

Moderately slow

1. Thou wilt come no more, gen - tle An - nie; like a
   roamed and loved 'mid the bow - ers when thy
   hours grow sad while I pon - der near the

flower, thy spir - it did de - part. Thou art gone, a - las! like the
down - y cheeks were in their bloom. Now I start a - lone 'mid the
si - lent spot where thou art laid, and my heart bows down when I

man - y that have bloomed in the sum - mer of my heart.
flow - ers while they min - gle their per - fume o'er thy tomb.
wan - der by the streams and the mead - ows where we strayed.

Shall we

never more be - hold thee nev - er hear thy win - ning voice a -

gain when the spring - time comes, gen - tle An - nie, when the

wild flowers are scat - tered o'er the plain?

1, 2

3

2. We have
3. Ah! the

rit.

I AM A PIRATE KING
from *The Pirates of Penzance*

W.S. Gilbert

Arthur Sullivan

mo - nious part, With a pi - rate head and a pi - rate heart.
ships, __ it's true, Than a well - bred mon - arch ought to do;

A - way to the cheat - ing
But man - y a king on a

world go you,
first - class throne,
Where
If he

pi - rates all __ are well - to - do; But I'll be true to the
wants to call __ his crown his own, Must man - age some - how

I WANT WHAT I WANT WHEN I WANT IT

from *Mlle. Modiste*

Henry Blossom

Victor Herbert

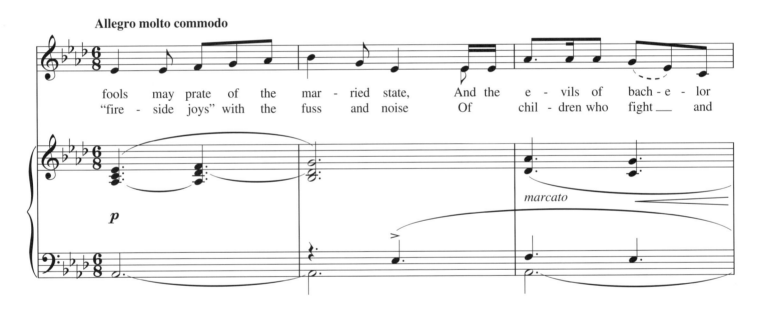

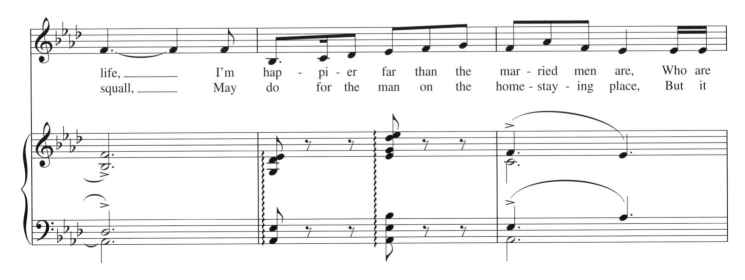

THE LAW IS THE TRUE EMBODIMENT

from *Iolanthe*

W.S. Gilbert

Arthur Sullivan

opt.
rath-er sus-cep-ti-ble Chan - cel-lor!

ff

p

But though the com - pli - ment im-plied In - flates me with le -

git - i - mate pride, It nev - er - the - less can't be de - nied, That it has its in - con -

ven - i - ent side. For I'm not so old, and not so plain, And I'm

quite pre- pared to mar- ry a- gain, But there'd be the deuce to pay in the Lords If I

fell in love with one of my Wards! Which

rath - er tries my tem - per, for I'm *such* a sus- cep - ti - ble Chan - ce- lor! Which

rath - er tries my tem - per, for I'm *such* a sus- cep - ti - ble Chan - cel- lor!

one for thou– and one for thee– But nev-er, oh nev-er a one for me!

Which is ex-as-per-at-ing, for A high-ly sus-cep-ti-ble

p

Chan - cel -lor! Which is ex-as - per - at - ing, for A high-ly sus-cep - ti - ble

f

Chan - cel -lor!

ff

THE MIDSHIPMITE

Fred E. Weatherly

Stephen Adams

1. 'Twas in fif - ty - five, on a
2. We launched the cut - ter, an'
3. "I'm done for now; good -

win - ter's night;   Cheer - i - ly, my lads, yo ho!   We'd
shoved her out;   Cheer - i - ly, my lads, yo ho!   The
bye," says he;   Stead - i - ly, my lads, yo ho!   You

got the Roosh - an lines in sight, When _ up comes a lit - tle
lub - bers might ha' heard us shout, As the Mid - dy ___ cried, "Now, my
make for the boat, nev - er mind for me!" "We'll _ take 'ee ___ back, sir, or

Mid - ship - mite; Cheer - i - ly, my lads, yo ho! ___
lads, put a -bout;" Cheer - i - ly, my lads, yo ho! We
die," says we; Cheer - i - ly, my lads, yo ho! So we

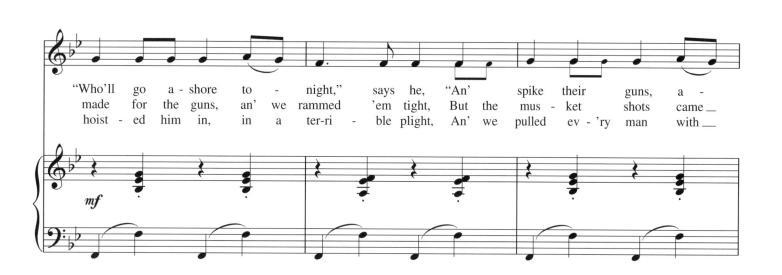

"Who'll go a - shore to - night," says he, "An' spike their guns, a -
made for the guns, an' we rammed 'em tight, But the mus - ket shots came _
hoist - ed him in, in a ter - ri - ble plight, An' we pulled ev - 'ry man with _

long wi' me?" "Why, ___ bless 'ee, ___ sir! come a - long," says we;
left and right, An' ___ down drops the poor lit - tle Mid - ship - mite;
all his might, An' ___ saved the ___ poor lit - tle Mid - ship - mite;

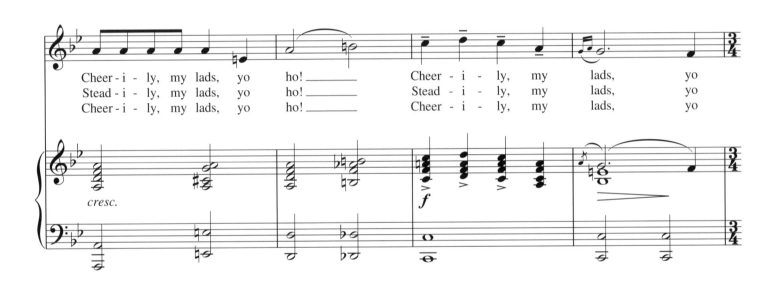

Cheer - i - ly, my lads, yo ho! _____ Cheer - i - ly, my lads, yo
Stead - i - ly, my lads, yo ho! _____ Stead - i - ly, my lads, yo
Cheer - i - ly, my lads, yo ho! _____ Cheer - i - ly, my lads, yo

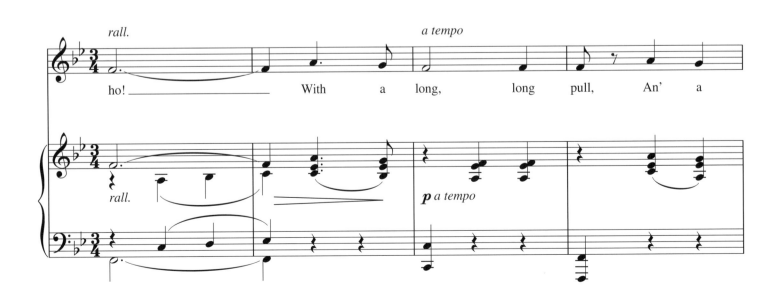

ho! _____ With a long, long pull, An' a

strong, strong pull, Gai - ly, boys, make ____ her go! ____ An' we'll drink to - night To the Mid - ship - mite, Sing - ing cheer - i - ly, lads, yo ho! ____ lads, yo ho! ____

MY GENEROUS HEART DISDAINS

Francis Hopkinson

NOTHING BUT A PLAIN OLD SOLDIER

Stephen C. Foster

Moderately fast

1. I'm noth - ing but a plain old sol - dier, an
friends I loved the best have de - part - ed, the
gain the bat - tle song is re - sound - ing, and

old rev - o - lu - tion - ar - y sol - dier, but I've han - dled a gun where
days of my ear - ly joys have gone, ___ and the voic - es once dear and fa -
who'll bring the trou - ble to an end? ___ The ___ U - nion will pout, and se -

no - ble deeds were done, for the name of my com - mand - er was George Wash - ing - ton. My
mil - iar to my ear have fad - ed from the scenes of the earth one by one. The
ces - sion ev - er shout, but none can tell us now which will yield or bend. You've

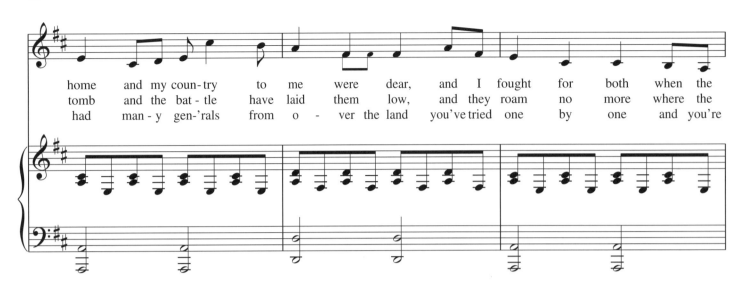

home   and my coun-try   to   me   were   dear,   and I fought   for   both   when the
tomb   and the bat-tle   have laid   them   low,   and they roam   no   more   where the
had   man-y gen-'rals   from o - ver the land   you've tried   one   by   one   and you're

ad lib.

foe   came   near,   but now   I will meet   with a   slight   or   sneer, for I'm
bright   streams   flow.   I'm long - ing to join   them and   soon   must   go, for I'm
still   at   a   stand,   but when I took the field   we had   one   in com-mand, yet I'm

colla voce

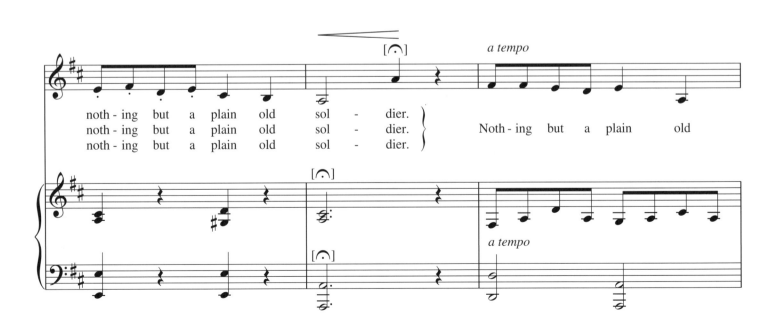

[⌢]

a tempo

noth - ing   but   a   plain   old   sol -   dier.
noth - ing   but   a   plain   old   sol -   dier.   Noth - ing   but   a   plain   old
noth - ing   but   a   plain   old   sol -   dier.

[⌢]

a tempo

sol - dier, an old rev - o - lu - tion - ar - y sol - dier, but I've

han - dled a gun where no - ble deeds were done, for the name of my com - mand - er was

George Wash - ing - ton.

1, 2

3

2. The
3. A -

THE OLD ROAD

Reginald V. Darow

John Prindle Scott

Straight and white, in the hot sun light, The __ high road stretch - es far; I hear the beat of the tramp - ing feet, Where the man - y trav - el - ers are; But my thoughts to - day fly

far, far a-way To a lit-tle wind-ing road, I knew, For my road is the old road, Where the sun lies warm and still, And my road is a by-road That winds up o-ver a hill; O, the high road is a long road, Where the

weary wayfarers roam; But I will take that little

winding road That leads the wanderer home!

Many a mile I have traveled the while, Through many a vale and

PUNCHINELLO

Fred E. Weatherly

James L. Molloy

He was a Pun - chi - nel - lo, Sweet Col - um - bine was she,
Bright was the day she mar - ried, And there a - mong the rest,

He loved the ground she danced on. She laughed his love to see;
Came poor old Pun - chi - nel - lo He was the blith - est guest.

poco più lento

Till he laughed him - self as gai - ly, Danc - ing, jok - ing ev' - ry night:
Had they seen his tears at mid - night, In his gar - ret near the sky,

opt.

poco più lento

a tempo

"He's the mad - dest, mer - riest fel - low!" Cried the peo - ple with de - light.
"He's the mad - dest, quaint - est fel - low!" That would still have been their cry.

a tempo

rall.

"Bra - vo! Bra - vo! Bra - vo! Bra - vo! Bra - vo! Pun - chi - nel - lo, Bra - vo Pun - chi - nel -

rall.

1

lo!"

a tempo

THE RAMBLING SAILOR

Collected and arranged by
Cecil J. Sharp

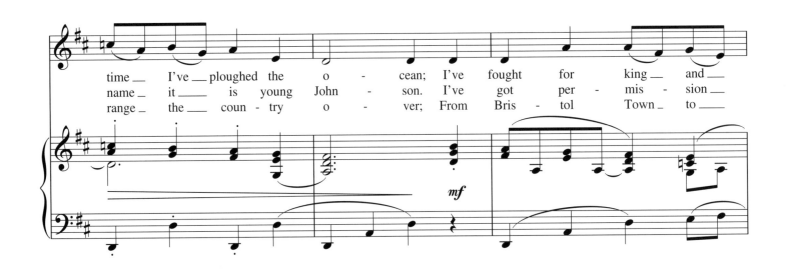

bid ___ you a - dieu, No more to the sea will I go with ___ you; I'll
will ___ you ___ do? Here's ale and ___ wine and ___ bran - dy ___ too; Be -
town ___ I ___ went, To court young ___ maid - ens ___ I was ___ bent; And

trav - el the coun - try ___ through and through, And I'll ___ be a ram - bling
sides a pair ___ of ___ new silk shoes, To trav - el with a ram - bling
mar - ry none ___ was ___ my in - tent, But live ___ a ___ ram - bling

1, 2
sail - or.
sail - or.

3
2. If
3. The

sail - or.

SHIPMATES O' MINE

Edward Teschemacher

Wilfred Sanderson

Maestoso

"Forth to the new land that ev - er is call - ing!" For - tune at - tend you there!

pesante

Good luck go with you! Ship - mates o' mine!

Tell me, tell me, where are you roam - ing, Ship - mates o'

THE SONG OF BROTHER HILARIO

Stephen Chalmers

Ralph Cox

way! But the kind am I that shall live and die, And be

glad he passed this way!

I like a book by the

in - gle nook, With a pipe and mulled old ale; To

THREE POOR MARINERS

Words Anonymous

Old English Melody
arranged by
Roger Quilter

Allegro con spirito e ben marcato ($\boldsymbol{d}$ = 80)

WHILE THE FOAMING BILLOWS ROLL

Thomas Linley

H. Lane Wilson

rall.

a tempo

Though to the Span-ish coast we're bound to steer, We'll still our rights main-

mf

tain, Then bear a hand, be stead-y, boys, Soon we'll see Old Eng-land once a-

cresc.

f

gain. From shore to shore, while can-nons

cresc.

f *ff*